Terms and Conditions

LEGAL NOTICE

The Publisher has strived to be as accurate and complete as possible in the creation of this report, notwithstanding the fact that he does not warrant or represent at any time that the contents within are accurate due to the rapidly changing nature of the Internet.

While all attempts have been made to verify information provided in this publication, the Publisher assumes no responsibility for errors, omissions, or contrary interpretation of the subject matter herein. Any perceived slights of specific persons, peoples, or organizations are unintentional.

In practical advice books, like anything else in life, there are no guarantees of income made. Readers are cautioned to reply on their own judgment about their individual circumstances to act accordingly.

This book is not intended for use as a source of legal, business, accounting or financial advice. All readers are advised to seek services of competent professionals in legal, business, accounting and finance fields.

You are encouraged to print this book for easy reading.

Table Of Contents

Foreword

Chapter 1:
Introduction To Article Marketing

Chapter 2:
Basics Of Article Marketing

Chapter 3:
The Resource Box

Chapter 4:
Writing Powerful Article Headlines

Chapter 5:
Article Copywriting Tips

Chapter 6:
SEO Article Writing

Chapter 7:
Article Marketing Mistakes To Avoid

Chapter 8:
The Road To Passive Traffic

Wrapping Up

Foreword

Traffic is the pre-requisite for any successful business. Just like how a typical brick and mortar shop needs people walking around to see their shop, an online business needs eyeballs as well.

The problem is that for many new entrepreneurs, they lack the financial budget or knowhow to generate tons of traffic for their businesses.

And then in the early internet marketing years, a group of people came up with the term "Article marketing" and this has been the forefront for free traffic generation till today.

Let's dwell deeper into this amazing phenomenon.

Article Wizard

Discover The Best Article Marketing Methods That Will Build Your Business On Steroids

Chapter 1:

Introduction To Article Marketing

Synopsis

Article Marketing is a method of generating traffic for your online business without any cost. Created early in the web 2.0 era, this method has been used ever since from marketers around the world to create online traffic streams till today.

Background

One of the good things about article marketing as it has the ability of creating **passive traffic.** Which means, you'll be getting traffic without having to actively be there. (We will see how in the next few chapters).

This seems like the ultimate choice especially for marketers who are on a shoestring budget. The essence of article marketing is that traffic generation relies on the articles content and SEO to draw traffic through search engines and from sites, which already have a huge following.

Article submission directories are places where people can submit articles to get more eyeballs for their websites. It is the bread and butter of using articles to draw traffic.

In the next section, we will look at the basics for drawing traffic through articles instantly.

Chapter 2:
Basics Of Article Marketing

Synopsis

Article marketing is a simple task. It requires a bit of hard work but if you can automate the process, generating traffic becomes much easier. That being said, let us see how it works.

The Basics

As mentioned earlier, you have to submit articles to article submission directories to generate traffic. Some of these article submission directories include:

-Ezine articles
-GoArticles
-Article Alley
-Article City

These websites or article directories already have a huge database of articles submitted by other marketers covering various topics from internet marketing to niche business and health articles. They already have a huge following so you can imagine the amount of traffic they get every day.

When you submit an article to them, you can get traffic through two ways:

1) These directories rank highly on Google. So if you target the right keywords, which aren't competitive (and must have many people searching for it), your article will appear on the search results fast.

2) These websites already have high traffic due to the number of people searching for information. Because of that, good articles will

often be featured on top of the article directories' featured section and you'll be tapping into this huge traffic source.

So what happens if someone sees your article? How does it generate traffic for you? We'll see how in the next section: The resource box!

Chapter 3:
The Resource Box

Synopsis

The resource box or author's bio box is a small box, which you can customize in the settings section of every article submission directory.

The Info

In this box, you can write a short bio about yourself and include one or two **self-serving links.** A self-serving link is basically a backlink to your website.

When someone reads your article and likes the content found, they can click on your link to find more articles. The amount of clicks you get from people who read your article would also depend on how good you craft your resource box, besides leveraging on the content of your article.

A good resource box must have 3 factors.

1) Establish credibility
2) Have a call to action or "bribe"
3) Contain self-serving links

You'll have to be able to talk about yourself without coming off as bragging and at the same time offer your readers something valuable so that they would click on your self-serving link. This could be something like a free e-book, e-course or more tips on something related to your niche articles.

Chapter 4:
Writing Powerful Article Headlines

Synopsis

The headline is probably the most important component of your article. Think about it, if you do not have a good headline, nobody is going to click on your article moreover click it. On top of that, if you do not target the keywords properly, nobody is going to be able to find your article because people find things based on keywords and key phrases.

Headlines

A smart thing to do would be to research important keywords related to your niche so you can target articles based on these keywords. You can start searching using the Google Keyword tool.

Furthermore, your article besides having keywords, must be able to grab your reader's attention. With the amount of articles and fluff available on the net, you'll need a good headline, which is striking and yet provides the valuable information to your readers.

Example: "5 Weight Loss Tips That Nutritionists Don't Know About".

What this title does is it targets the keyword weight loss tips and yet is able to strike readers attention because something that even nutritionists don't know about might be worth reading.

Here's a good exercise: Brainstorm 10-50 article titles you think would be able to attract attention and target good keywords.

Chapter 5:
Article Copywriting Tips

Synopsis

Copywriting is the art of getting your readers to carry out your most desired action. This could be something from getting them to click on a link, sign up to your mailing list or even buy a product.

Some Tips

In the context of article marketing, your job is to get them to do two things:

1) Fall in love with your content
2) Click on your self-serving links

There are a few things you can do here:

1) The first is the optimizing your headlines (refer to chapter 4). Remember, the body content of your article must relate to your article title.
2) Use bullet points to lay out key points and elaborate on them.
3) Give examples. Illustrating examples helps get the ideas across more clearly.
4) Ask questions. Asking questions gets their mind juice flowing and more involved in your articles.

In short, follow these simple guidelines and you'll be on the road to them getting to click on your links and getting massive traffic to your website.

Chapter 6:
SEO Article Writing

Synopsis

SEO stands for search engine optimization, which is the art of getting your articles found on the search engines. The current largest search engine in the world is Google, so you'll need to know what Google likes in web content to be able to get your articles found.

SEO

The first thing you must know about SEO, is that you must be very clear with the keywords you are trying to target. High search volume + less competition would be a good guide. In short, don't exceed 2% worth of keyword density for your articles.

Don't just target main keywords, you can try long tail keywords (keywords with less search volume but virtually zero competition). These searches are normally highly targeted and these guys could probably be your buying customers.

If you want to include a link in your body text (see if your submission directory allows it), make sure you use anchor text links – Meaning that the words for the link is actually a keywords. E.g. if you want to link to your dog training website, an anchor text link would be "dog training tips"

The best thing about SEO, is that it doesn't matter if you are submitting it to article directories, the same works for article you put on your own blog, other people's blogs or basically any form of web content! One more thing... Google is getting smarter and smarter so content is equally important as SEO.

Chapter 7:

Article Marketing Mistakes To Avoid

Synopsis

Article marketing can be a very powerful tool for generating massive passive traffic. But if you use it incorrectly, you'll end up doing more harm than benefits. Here are some article marketing mistakes you should avoid at all cost:

The Errors

1) Over-doing the keywords. If you put too much keywords in your article for SEO purposes, you'll end up coming off as spam by Google and this will hurt your rankings. Furthermore
2) Not optimizing your resource box. A lot of views are left on the table because people fail to optimize their resource box. A call to action must be followed by a self-serving link
3) Grammatical errors. This is a huge no-no and is shunned by article submission directories. Check your spelling and grammar at all times in Microsoft word before submitting.
4) Too short word count/too long word count. Let's face it, short articles don't cut it for most directories and long articles are a hassle to read. People's attention span is short.

In short, success in article writing lies in adhering to good writing practices and avoiding silly mistakes. Don't forget, content and SEO are king so you have to place a huge focus on those as well, while not overlooking the small stuff.

Chapter 8:

The Road To Passive Traffic

Synopsis

Article marketing gives a great way to generate traffic, and that being said, you won't get traffic instantly by submitting a few articles. The process to traffic building via article marketing is a long one, and you'll have to consistently produce good articles, which meet standards and also is up to date with relevant information.

How To Get There

That being said, how does one generate passive traffic through articles? There are a few ways. For one, you can hire a ghostwriter to post articles for you. This cuts you out of the equation and can give you more time to focus on the marketing aspects of your business.

You can also pay to have your articles featured in websites or directories. This is a faster way to get a boost in your traffic by having your featured article put in front of the website.

Another way is to master SEO (or if you have the money, hire someone whose good in it) to optimize your web content so that the SEO will bring in long term steady passive traffic for your website.

Finally, you might consider partnering with someone. That someone will do the article-writing portion while you focus on the other aspects such as creating products, marketing etc.

Wrapping Up

Traffic generation is a tedious process, but can be enjoyable if you have the passion to learn and give to your followers.

Article marketing is great way, especially for young businesses to get their niche business up and running.

A smart marketer knows how to utilize all sorts of traffic generation options. Perhaps with the money made from your passive article traffic, you might want to invest in some paid traffic methods so to double your traffic and double your profits.

Finally, you should always consider cutting yourself out of the equation so that you can enjoy a passive income without having to work. As Robert Kiyosaki says, the most successful people are the investors (not business managers).

I wish you all the best in your article marketing success!

Wrapping Up

Traffic generation is a tedious process, but can be enjoyable if you have the passion to learn and give to your followers.

Article marketing is great way, especially for young businesses to get their niche business up and running.

A smart marketer knows how to utilize all sorts of traffic generation options. Perhaps with the money made from your passive article traffic, you might want to invest in some paid traffic methods so to double your traffic and double your profits.

Finally, you should always consider cutting yourself out of the equation so that you can enjoy a passive income without having to work. As Robert Kiyosaki says, the most successful people are the investors (not business managers).

I wish you all the best in your article marketing success!

www.ingramcontent.com/pod-product-compliance
Lightning Source LLC
Chambersburg PA
CBHW031511210526
45463CB00008B/3197